The spiritual path . . . is simply the journey of living our lives.
Everyone is on a spiritual path; most people just don't know it.

Marianne Williamson

Life is really about a spiritual unfolding that is personal and enchanting—an unfolding that no science or philosophy or religion has yet fully clarified.

James Redfield

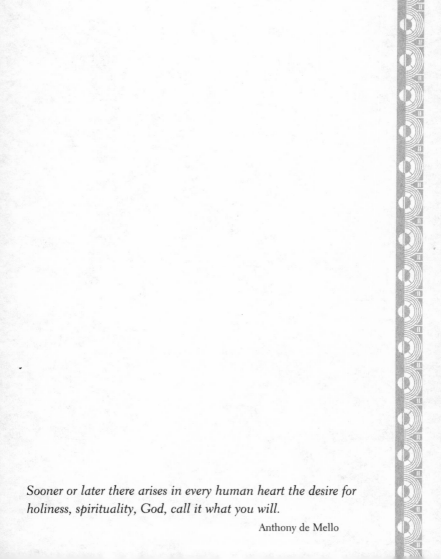

Sooner or later there arises in every human heart the desire for holiness, spirituality, God, call it what you will.

Anthony de Mello

There is a spiritual realm that is available to all who find its many entrances.

James Melvin Washington

Spiritual life is like a moving sidewalk. Whether you go with it or spend your whole life running against it, you're still going to be taken along.

Bernadette Roberts

We are not human beings learning to be spiritual; we are spiritual beings learning to be human.

Jacquelyn Small

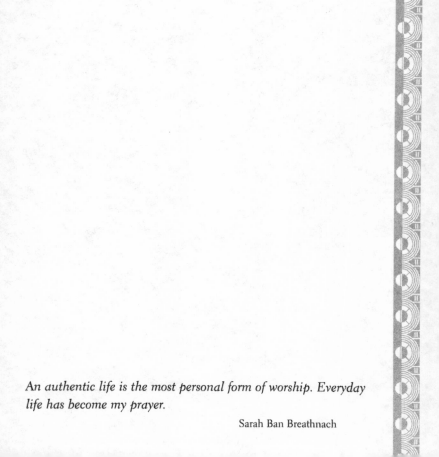

An authentic life is the most personal form of worship. Everyday life has become my prayer.

Sarah Ban Breathnach

What you are is God's gift to you; what you make of it is your gift to God.

Anthony Dalla Villa

In the faces of men and women I see God.

Walt Whitman

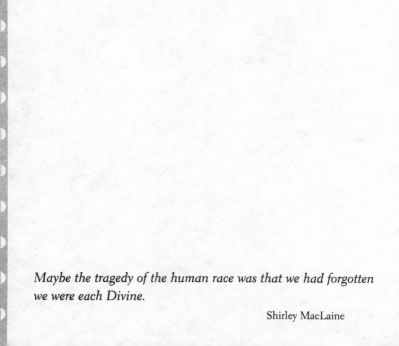

Maybe the tragedy of the human race was that we had forgotten we were each Divine.

Shirley MacLaine

Prayer is a long rope with a strong hold.

Harriet Beecher Stowe

Prayer is the language of the heart.

Grace Aguilar

No sincere prayer leaves us where it finds us.

Stella Terrill Mann

The wish to pray is prayer in itself.

Georges Bernanos

It could not happen that any man or woman could pray for a single moment without some good result.

Alexis Carrel

We're not human beings that have occasional spiritual experiences—it's the other way around: we're spiritual beings that have occasional human experiences.

Deepak Chopra

For all that has been—Thanks! To all that shall be—Yes!

Dag Hammarskjöld

One single, thankful thought directed to heaven is the most perfect prayer.

Gotthold Ephraim Lessing

To those leaning on the sustaining infinite, today is big with blessings.

Mary Baker Eddy

Ask, and you will receive. Seek, and you will find. Knock, and it will be opened to you.

Jesus of Nazareth

A prayer in its simplest definition is merely a wish turned Godward.

Phillips Brooks

All our acts have sacramental possibilities.

Freya Stark

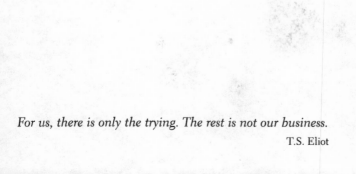

For us, there is only the trying. The rest is not our business.

T.S. Eliot

There are many, many gates to the sacred and they are as wide as we need them to be.

Sherry Ruth Anderson and Patricia Hopkins

There is only one journey. Going inside yourself.

Rainer Maria Rilke

If we go down into ourselves we find that we possess exactly what we desire.

Simone Weil

If you do not go within, you go without.

Neale Donald Walsch

The externals are simply so many props; everything we need is within us.

Etty Hillesum

All you need is deep within you waiting to unfold and reveal itself. All you have to do is be still and take time to seek for what is within, and you will surely find it.

Eileen Caddy

Every time you don't follow your inner guidance, you feel a loss of energy, loss of power, a sense of spiritual deadness.

Shakti Gawain

This whole world is full of God!

Blessed Angela of Foligno

i found god in myself
& i loved her
i loved her fiercely.

Ntozake Shange

Be fervent in God, and let nothing grieve you, whatever you encounter.

Hadewijch

A Soul is partly given, partly wrought.

Erica Jong

It is not that we have a soul, *we* are *a soul.*

Amelia E. Barr

The soul is partly in eternity and partly in time.

Marsilio Ficino

Those who see any difference between soul and body have neither.

Oscar Wilde

The divorce of our so-called spiritual life from our daily activities is a fatal dualism.

M.P. Follett

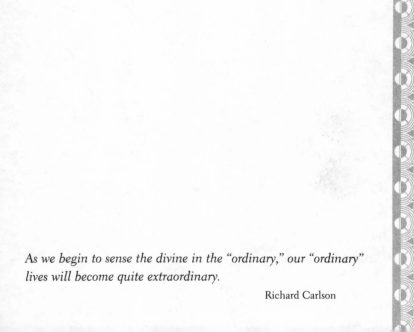

As we begin to sense the divine in the "ordinary," our "ordinary" lives will become quite extraordinary.

Richard Carlson

If I find in myself a desire which no experience in this world can satisfy, the most probable explanation is that I was made for another world.

C.S. Lewis

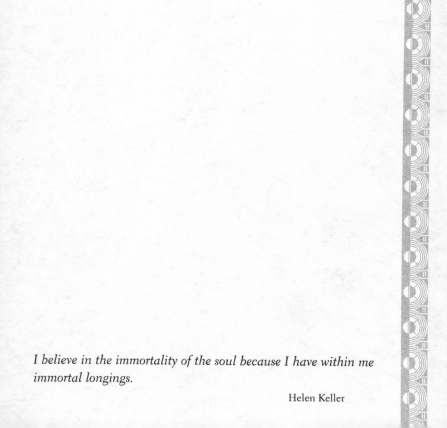

I believe in the immortality of the soul because I have within me immortal longings.

Helen Keller

Every day is a god, each day is a god, and holiness holds forth in time.

Annie Dillard

True spirituality does not exist without love of life.

Nathaniel Branden

To the soul, the ordinary is sacred and the everyday is the primary source of religion.

Thomas Moore

My soul can find no staircase to Heaven unless it be through Earth's loveliness.

Michelangelo

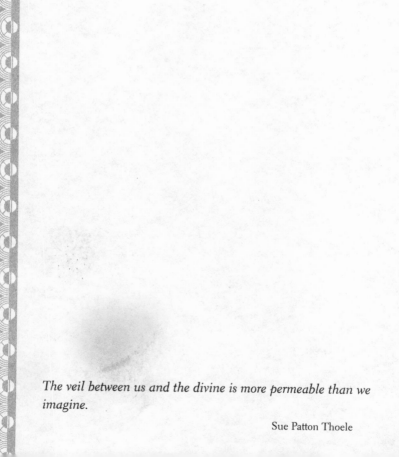

The veil between us and the divine is more permeable than we imagine.

Sue Patton Thoele

The flesh is as spiritual as the soul, and the soul is as natural as the flesh.

Jane Roberts

Your daily life is your temple and your religion.
Whenever you enter into it take with you your all.

Kahlil Gibran

There is no enlightenment outside daily life.

Thich Nhat Nanh

Awareness of the sacred in life is what holds our world together, and the lack of awareness of the sacred is what is tearing it apart.

Joan Chittister

The dramatic action that we need to create a way of life on Earth that really works will be taken not through personal, social, or political action, but through spiritual action.

Brooke Medicine Eagle

Spiritual life is a matter of becoming who you truly are. It's not becoming Catherine of Siena, or some other saint, but who you are. It sounds easy enough, but being who you truly are is work, courage and faith.

Richard Rohr

I never went to bed in my life and I never ate a meal in my life without saying a prayer. I know my prayers have been answered thousands of times, and I know that I never said a prayer in my life without something good coming of it.

Jack Dempsey

Holiness is not a luxury for the few; it is not just for some people. It is meant for you and for me and for all of us. It is a simple duty, because if we learn to love, we learn to be holy.

Mother Teresa

PRENTICE HALL
Career & Personal Development
Paramus, NJ 07652
A Simon & Schuster Company

On the World Wide Web at http://www.phdirect.com